T0171445

EEEZ MEDITATION FOR BEGINNERS

Empowerment with EEEZ

Marjolyn Noble and Leon Steed

BALBOA.
PRESS

A DIVISION OF HAY HOUSE

Balboa Press books may be ordered through booksellers or by contacting:

Balboa Press
A Division of Hay House
1663 Liberty Drive
Bloomington, IN 47403
www.balboapress.com.au
1-(877) 407-4847

ISBN: 978-1-4525-0873-3 (sc)
ISBN: 978-1-4525-0874-0 (e)

Printed in the United States of America

Balboa Press rev. date: 2/1/2013

Contents

Introduction to Meditation

Welcome to EEEZ Meditation for Beginners. Together we will go on a mental journey where you can enjoy, relax, and release any unwanted tensions and emotions. When you embrace meditation on a regular basis, whether it is daily, weekly, or with a group, the benefits that you may gain are plenty. Meditation can have the following benefits:

- Reduction in stress
- More confidence
- Increased focus and concentration
- Increased acceptance of self
- Changes in attitude towards life
- Improved ability to focus
- Increased creativity
- Deeper level of relaxation
- Improved perception and memory
- Natural change in breathing
- Decrease in stress hormone
- Lower blood pressure
- Reversal of the aging process
- Reduction in cholesterol
- Increased self-actualization
- Increased strength of self-concept
- Decreased cigarette, alcohol, and drug abuse
- Increased productivity

- Improved relations at work
- Improved health and more positive health habits

The list goes on, and the benefits to you will be as individual as you are. What you focus on, you will create.

It is recommended that you create a space in your home or wherever you choose to meditate. Make this place your "meditation place." When you meditate regularly, you will be able to enter the relaxation state quickly and easily as you connect with your "sacred space." You may like to place some crystals or flowers or something symbolic in your place to enhance your experience. Choose a comfortable chair that will support your back, or sit on a pillow and lean against a wall. It is recommended that you sit rather than lie down, as you may fall asleep, which is not the ideal outcome. Perhaps you might like to set an alarm, just in case.

Allow yourself at least fifteen minutes; this is your time. Congratulations on your decision to give something back to *you*.

The following will assist you to get the most out of your mediation experience: Breathe slowly and deeply. Close your eyes softly. Begin by taking a few slow and deep breaths—inhaling with your nose and exhaling from your mouth. Don't force your breathing. Let it come naturally. Fill your lungs and exhale as deeply as you can. Take as long as you need to breathe slowly and deeply.

How to Use This Book: Prepare Yourself

S tep 1—Choose a meditation that appeals to you.

Step 2—Read the contents several times to familiarise yourself with the emotion.

Step 3—Put on some relaxation music.

Step 4—Read the breathing technique instructions below to help bring you into a state of relaxation.

Get into a comfortable position where you will be free from any distractions for the next fifteen minutes. Take the phone off the hook and put your cell phone on silent. When you are ready, close your eyes and take a long deep breath in through your nose, filling you lungs completely and slowly breathing out through your mouth to the count of five—1, 2, 3, 4, 5. Breathe in—1, 2, 3. Breathe out—1, 2, 3, 4, 5. Allow yourself to feel relaxed with every breath in—1, 2, 3.

Make this your time to relax and to allow your subconscious mind to make some positive changes. Focus on the words. If your mind starts to wander, that's all right, but bring yourself back and keep focused on the words. Feel more and more relaxed with each breath in. Notice your muscles loosen and tension disappear. Feel more at peace.

Starting at your feet, begin tensing them tightly and then release, feeling the ease that is now descending upon you. Focus on the words, and breathe out any tension, any negativity, any doubt. Breathe in ... breathe out ... breathe in ... breathe out. Focus on the words. Breathe in and breathe out. Feel more and more relaxed and at peace.

Breathe deeply, exhale completely, and focus. Working your way up your body, tense your muscles and release, feeling more relaxed with every breath.

Awareness: When you are breathing deeply, you'll begin to feel calmer and more relaxed. That's perfect for you at this moment. Now focus your attention on your breathing. Be aware of each breath that you take in through your nose. When inhaling, aim for the count of three. Be mindful of each breath that you exhale with your mouth; aim for the count of five. Continue focusing on your breath.

If you find your attention straying away from your breath, just gently bring it back. Don't be discouraged. What's important is realizing that you've wandered and bringing your attention back to where it should be. As you develop greater focus power, you will find it easier to concentrate.

Ending the session: When you are ready to end the session, open your eyes and stand up slowly. You may get so relaxed, time will slip by faster than you anticipate. Stretch yourself and extend your increased awareness to your next activities. You've done it! Well done!

Remember that everyone's experience with meditation will be different, and that is how it's meant to be. There is no right or wrong way; there is only *your* way. Enjoy what comes to you.

If you prefer an audio version to guide you, visit *www. easemedititationonline.com* and download a track onto your smartphone or MP3 player.

Guided Meditations— Visualisations

---◆·◆·◆---

Accessing Your Intuition

Do you feel it? Do you hear it? Sit very still and take note of your breath. Feel your chest rising up and then dropping down. Take a deep breath in, deep breath out—breathe in deeply, exhale fully.

Sitting in a comfortable position, close your eyes and focus your attention inward (refer to the breathing technique on page ix-x).

Imagine a lovely place where you feel completely relaxed, without a worry in the world. You're happy and carefree. Take a look around you and notice the details of your surroundings. What can you see? What can you smell? What can you hear? Most importantly, what can you feel?

For the next ten to fifteen minutes make it your intention to focus on being completely in the moment; you don't need to be anywhere. You feel very much at peace, and you're calming your mind. You are completely absorbed in the lovely atmosphere of your surroundings, enjoying all the beautiful sights and sounds.

Visualize a beautiful field, with soft velvety grass, see yourself seated in the lovely setting. The green grass is so brilliant; it is emerald-like, and the smell is that crisp grass scent that invigorates the very core of your being. Take a long, slow, lingering look at your environment. See the beautiful sights of this wonderful, picturesque setting. Capture the detail in your mind, create a blueprint of this, and store it internally so you can return at any time.

Now turn your attention to how you feel. When was the last time you felt this calm and serene?

Take a few moments now to relax, just be at peace, savour the moment.

Did you know that you have an internal guidance system? It is very much like a personalized navigator. It is otherwise known as your emotions. The purpose of these emotions is to guide you continually to a place of contentment. This is accomplished by being aware of how and what you are feeling. Achieving awareness permits you to always return to a calm and relaxed presence, regardless of the situation you may find yourself in during the course of our day.

Our emotional guidance system is our gift from the Universe while we are here on planet Earth. It is our GPS to keep us on the path to joy and happiness. We are never alone, and it is through our emotions that our higher self, Source Energy, Guardian Angel (whatever title you are comfortable with) speaks to us. Source lets us know how we are feeling at any given moment. When we are not on our path to joy, we feel negative emotions, which are our indicator to change what we are thinking. That is all we need to do—change our thoughts.

Now, take some time to speak with your loving Guidance and trust the words that follow. Feel the love and see the beautiful, vivid flow of liquid light that pours directly into your core, your centre, your heart. Breathe deeply this light of love and feel your expansion.

Take eight to ten minutes for silent reflection.

Trust is the lesson for us all. We can trust that our internal guidance, or intuition, will always lead us down the right path, and we will know when we feel good. If there is a negative feeling, it is only our Guidance System alerting us to change our direction to one that feels better. That is all we need to do.

Now, trust the next few words that come to you, bring back some guidance for your day, and trust that the words that flow will be the perfect words you need now. Trust your guidance.

Awareness

You have just awakened from a very peaceful sleep, and to your surprise, you are not in your bed but standing in front of a majestic temple. This building has been hand carved out of marble; the details of carvings, which adorn these walls, are brilliant works of art. Gifted sculptors and artists from days gone by—the likes of Michelangelo, da Vinci, and Picasso—have shaped this building. They have all come together to create a masterpiece like no other. Take a long, glorious look at this magnificent work of art, and marvel at the intricacy of the detail: all hand chiselled from the purest white marble, mother-of-pearl sheen, glowing so brightly, sparkling like stars in the universal sky.

As you walk around the temple, you feel with each step that your awareness is enhanced. You notice the minute details; the workmanship of these masters is a wonder to behold. Soon you are standing at the entrance of this temple, where massive timber doors are engraved with the most glorious carvings. There are thousands of pearls embedded into the timber, and they are so magnificent, it leaves you in awe. Just absorb the beauty, craftsmanship, and creativity of these masters.

You notice a sign above the door, welcoming you to the Temple of Enhanced Awareness. Knock on the door, and hear echoes that reverberate throughout the temple—deep bass tones that awaken all your senses. You are feeling vibrant.

The doors glide open with ease, and you see yourself stepping into a foyer. The space is so large, it defies logic. However, with your new awareness, you realise this is an illusion—one that you have created. This space is the freedom you seek, the space you can come to when you need to have awareness and clarity. It is free from clutter and distraction and doubt.

As you stand in this space, all that was unknown to you is now crystal clear; you know that you have the answer to every question here. Just like finding the missing pieces from a jigsaw puzzle, you now find you have the complete picture. You come to the realisation that, with awareness, you can change whatever is not working for you; all it takes is some clarity and awareness.

Instantly, you feel what's been missing in your life. Self-love fills every cell of your being. And self-appreciation has been heightened with your new sense of awareness; it feels so natural and complete. You understand without judgement that everything that has happened to you up to today has shaped you, made you who you are, just like the creation of this magical temple.

With this enhanced awareness, you understand that the past is just that; however, you can control your thoughts of now, which in turn will create what comes to you. What you think, so you will become. You now know, without any doubt, how loved you are and have always been. With crystal-clear understanding, you realise that any limits have been self-imposed, and now you have the power to create a future so bright that your every wish can be realised. There is nothing that you cannot be. You realise with happiness that you can never go back. You now have access to wisdom and guidance from the same source that creates galaxies.

Stay in the magical foyer for a while and contemplate what you are able to achieve with this newfound awareness and clarity.

Butterfly Guided Meditation

Find a space where you can sit in peace with no distractions. Make the next ten to fifteen minutes a special time just for you, one where you can connect with your higher self, your inner being.

Sitting in a comfortable position, close your eyes and focus your attention inward (refer to the breathing technique on page ix-x).

Feeling very relaxed and at peace, imagine yourself standing on the edge of a rainforest, the most beautiful setting you can image. The energy you feel is one of calm. You are at one with nature, totally at ease and absorbing the healing energy that comes from such a magical place. Take in all the sights and really notice the details. Look closely at the intricate patterns provided by nature on the leaves of ferns. Look up towards the sky and see the sunlight filtering through the tops of the trees. See a golden beam of sunlight coming down and shining all around and over you. Take a deep breath of this energy, revitalising your cells, lifting your spirit. With each inhalation, you grow more and more radiant.

Notice the path to your right. Start walking into the forest. Hear the crunch of the path beneath your feet. With each step forward, your awareness of the surroundings becomes more pronounced. Feel the energy, see the beauty, and hear the sounds of the insects and animals of the rainforest. Stop and look at the fern tree to your left; there's a green tree frog. And over to the right there is a bush turkey pecking at the soil. This is a perfect ecosystem buzzing with life.

As you move along the path, observe the minute details, hear the peaceful sounds, and notice the feeling of serenity that permeates your being. The deeper into the forest you go, the more beauty you see. It sparkles; it shines. It is such a place of wonder and delight. It is perfect in every way.

Wow, do you see the butterflies? There are *so* many now appearing, with colours so bright—from sky blue, to teal, to turquoise. And the shapes! There are so many varieties. You have never experienced anything like this before. Look in awe and appreciation at the show Mother Nature is sharing with you. Notice their ease as they flitter gently through the environment. You feel as light and graceful as these butterflies, as though you are floating down the path deeper into the forest. You are totally at peace and in harmony; the connection is complete. Take your time; enjoy the walk.

You come to a clearing in the forest where there is a tepee. This is a sacred tepee just for you. Inside is a book entitled *Knowledge of All That Is.* On the pages of this book are the answers to every question that has ever been asked, and the answer to your question is in there too. Go ahead. Enter this sacred place and sit down. Feel the love as you enter. Feel the joy that you have found in this beautiful place. Feel the contentment that is you, and know that you are completely loved and safe. Smell the sage sticks that are burning, feel the softness of the grass under your feet, and see the magic light within the tepee. Your sense of well-being is heightened to levels that you are experiencing for the first time.

Now that you are seated, reach over and place the book in your arms. Hug the book and feel the knowledge pouring into your being. Think of the question that you would like answered. Trust whatever comes into your mind, as this is question that is perfect for you right now. Trust that this is what you have been waiting to hear.

I will leave you here for a few moments to ponder the question. When you feel the time is right, open the book to any page and look down; your answer will be before you. Trust the message that you hear, see, or feel. Trust that this is right for you at this moment. Trust. ...

Take five minutes to reflect on the words you have just read,

When you are ready, place the book down and give thanks to All That Is for sharing the wisdom and guidance, and know that your answer has been given to you. It is now time to leave the tepee and head back into the forest and start the return journey back.

As you leave, you are returning with a new sense of purpose, knowing that you can return to this magical place any time you desire. Walking slowly, you are now feeling confident and peaceful. With every step you are feeling more alert and alive; with every step you feel more awake. Start by wriggling your toes, your fingers. Feel your new alertness. Wiggle your arms, roll your shoulders, stretch. ... You are ready to come back to now, feeling fresh, rejuvenated, happy, and content.

Corporate Environment Meditation

S ee the oxygen inside your body after you inhale, filling your body
gently. Notice how you feel as you take each new breath in. You are
feeling more energised and lighter. Any tension that may have come
your way has been released, and you feel inspired for what is coming.
You have a clear mind and can see easily how much enjoyment you
have for your work. See yourself embracing each task with a renewed
sense of achievement, and it feels great. You know that you have access
to an abundance of resources—all within you. All you need to do
to access them is take a few minutes of reflective thought—and the
solution appears. You realise that your thoughts are in harmony with
your feelings, and when you feel good, your day flows. Colleagues
will feel your energy and follow your lead. It's so wonderful to lead by
example.

Take another breath in; feel your chest and stomach gently rise and fall with each breath. You feel vibrant; you feel alive; you feel like there is no obstacle on your path. You know that you can come to this feeling any time you choose to focus on feeling good.

Now you are feeling very light after releasing tension that may have come up during the course of your work. You are ready to come back, ready to complete whatever activity requires your attention with the knowledge that it will all proceed smoothly.

Feel how calm and gentle your breathing is. Now it is time to return your body and mind back into the room. Keeping your eyes closed, become aware of the sounds around you. Feel yourself seated in your chair. Wiggle your fingers and toes, shrug your shoulders. Now slowly open your eyes and spend a short time absorbing this feel-good energy. Stretch out your arms and legs, and when you're ready, stand up. Look around at your surroundings; see how things look clearer and crisper with this new energy you have.

Enjoy the rest of your day. You created this feeling, and now you can experience the benefits that come with it.

Happiness Meditation

Take a few deep breathes in through your nose and out through your mouth, breathe in, breathe out, breathe in breathe out, repeat several times. Now that you are feeling very calm, just take your attention to a time when you felt really happy. Recall that time, what were you doing, who you were with. Replay that image in your mind, feel the emotion, hear the laughter, enjoy. When you are feeling in a happy state, you are vibrating energy for others to feel. This energy ripples out and through your happiness, you have the ability to touch someone else.

You understand that you are the only person responsible for your happiness—you and only you. With this loving knowledge you are empowered into action for your own well-being. You are no longer looking for external sources of this emotion; you understand that it is entirely up to you. Happiness is perception—it's how you interpret an event.

Take a moment to feel happy. What does happiness mean to you? Is it spending time in the sun? Or is it walking with your dog or enjoying the company of your children? Happiness is unique to you.

Now turn your attention to a time when you laughed so much, your sides ached. Imagine this again and feel the warmth of this moment, feel the wave of love that is coming deep from within you. This is your spirit, soul, or whatever name you feel comfortable with. This spirit loves you unconditionally, just as you are. You are perfect. This is the true happiness that you seek: embracing the love of who you are. Being happy as *you*—when you find peace with who you are right now—you can embrace a whole new world with a new outlook. You no longer look externally for your happiness; you no longer require your partner, child, sibling, or friend to be the source of your happiness

I will now leave you with your thoughts for a while. Enjoy your "happy space." Turn to your spirit and enjoy some quiet time together. Feel the love and joy that flows to you.

Take seven to ten minutes for reflection.

By turning your attention to happy memories at times when life is a bit more challenging, you are able to move your emotions to a lighter space. This in turn brings more memories and feelings of relief. This is the key to your happiness: awareness that it is up to you, that you can change your thoughts any time to ones of happiness or to something softer to take your focus off the unwanted.

The Miracle of Creation—*You*

To begin, close your eyes, relax, and take a deep breath. Refer to the steps on how to prepare page ix-x

Take a moment to go inwards and just *be*. Reflect on the beautiful creation which is *you*. Can you appreciate the beauty of *you?* Can you be grateful for the wonderful *you* that you've become. Do you see how better this Universe is because of *you?* Everyone you have met, talked with, worked with, or laughed with is richer because of *you*. *You* are a unique creation from the same Source that made this Universe; you are as miraculous as the Milky Way and beyond. Each of us has been given the wonderful opportunity of life, to be here at this time. Value each breath of air you inhale. Value every waking moment that you get to share on this magnificent planet. Value the contribution you are making. There is no measurement required; any contribution in any way is valid.

Now go into a relaxed state. Just relax, just enjoy, and just be at peace. You don't need to think about what is about to be said. Just muse on it, play with it, let it in. No deep thoughts are required, for the moment. Worry, struggle, stress, strife, obstacles, problems—these are things that are outside the reality you are now in. Just feel your existence and appreciate your existence; feel how good it is to exist, to be alive, to be aware.

I exist. I am existence. I am what is. I am what I am. I need no reason for I am already here. I need no excuse for I am already here. I need no rationale for I am already here. Is'ness is my being. Is'ness is my birth right. Is'ness is my fundamental nature. *I AM.* There is absolute knowing in this statement. Allow yourself to feel that absolute, unquestionable certainty that you exist. Take a deep breath and say, "I AM." It is to this degree that all knowing must be experienced, for if you have the same effect in manifesting in your life, and even when, and even if you experience the idea of fear and you experience the idea of doubt, go back to a state of absolute *I AM.* Rekindle that state; realign that state within you. … I AM. … Take a deep breath and say, "I AM."

Letting Go

This journey is all about letting go: letting go of doubt, letting go of fear, letting go of negativity. It is all about trust and allowing wonderful feelings to replace the emotions you are releasing. Imagine yourself standing by a river. The water is flowing and a gentle breeze blowing. It is a perfect spring day. The sun is bright. The flowers that line the river's edge are in full bloom; the scent is sweet and fills the air. Birds are singing, insects chattering, bees humming.

Breathe this ambience in. You are feeling very tranquil and grateful to be enjoying this environment. Now reach deep into your pockets, and one at time, take out the emotional rock that is weighing on your mind. Hold the rock in both hands, and label it with the negative feeling that you want to let go. See the emotional name appearing on the surface and say to yourself as you throw the rock into the river, "I release you as you no longer have a place in my life. I am now free to choose how I feel and I choose to feel great.

Reach deep into your pockets again and take the next rock out. Throw this into the river just like the last one, and let go of the emotion that no longer serves you. Keep doing this until your pockets are empty and you feel light. The weight that has been holding you down is no longer there. See yourself standing taller, brighter and happier—even joyous—as you feel the relief and release of those unwanted emotions.

Take a walk along the river's edge and notice the carvings in the trees. They have been placed there as a reminder to you of all the beautiful feelings you have created space for: love, gratitude, appreciation, wonder, anticipation. Your sense of freedom is now at an all-time high. You are now free to embrace life and all the wonders that come your way. You now easily recognise when a negative emotion comes along and with your newfound awareness you replace it with a thought that makes you feel good. It could be something as simple as recalling a beautiful smile that you saw or a pleasing memory. With your new found sense of calm, you realise how free you are to create whatever you desire. How you feel *does* matter, and you choose to feel good. It is all up to you; only you can decide how you feel—and you choose happiness. You know that you are never alone; there are caring souls who are with you always.

Take some time now to reflect on a wonderful new beginning you are creating by releasing the negative emotions that no longer serve you. Live the fulfilling life you intend to create. Start visualising a life you want. Everything we live takes shape as a thought first, by placing our focus on whatever outcome we choose it will become a creation, good or otherwise.

Enjoy some time to reflect, focus on the outcome of your desires.

Now I would like you to go into the future, into a time that has not yet been. See yourself living a peaceful and serene life, where doubt, fear and negativity are no longer a part of your existence. What are you saying to yourself, what are you seeing, and what are you feeling? The lesson you learnt by the river that day and the messages carved into the trees are now a part of your daily existence. You wake up every morning and before getting out of bed, you give thanks for the beautiful day that is about to begin. Every day is an opportunity for a new start; every day is a day to give thanks for. Give thanks for being alive, for the wonderful people you connect with, for the food you eat, for the clean clothes you wear—for the simple things that give you so much pleasure.

It is a blessed life you are living and your smile lights up for everyone to see. You're feeling so light, so fresh and so vibrant that others look at you and sense your well-being. You are a glowing example of a contented person. How wonderful is that?! Spend a few moments basking in this feeling.

Let's anchor this sensation so you can recall this feeling any time you wish. Gently squeeze the tip of your little finger on your right hand and at the same time feel the sense of calm and tranquillity. Hold for the count of three, and then gently release. Squeeze again whilst feeling at peace, knowing that whenever you want to you can squeeze your little finger and instantly feel at peace. What a gift to give to yourself!

It is time to come back to now. When you are ready, gently move your feet, your legs, and your arms, feeling more alert with each movement. Know that the awareness you are brining into your now moment gives you a real sense of purpose.

Coming back now, you are feeling more alert, ready to embrace whatever you choose to do. Open your eyes and you are now feeling very refreshed and fantastic. Well done. Remember that whenever you want to recall the beautiful sense of well-being, gently squeeze your right little finger.

New Perspective

This mediation is recommended for the start of your day.

See yourself standing on a beautiful tropical beach with the softest white sand, silky smooth beneath your feet. The tiny granules gently massage the souls of your feet, sending a quiver right through your body. It feels luxurious, velvety, sensuous and so relaxing and calming. Look out to ocean and marvel at the picturesque, brilliant blue waters gently lapping at the shore. A very light breeze brushes your cheeks, you feel very relaxed. Enjoy the moment. The water is *so* inviting. The tropical trees that line the beach are gently swaying. You have this entire beach all to yourself. Take time to look around and notice the beauty; lie down and stretch out; bask in the delightful sunlight. This is the best sensation you can feel. Run your hands through the soft sand; it is so soothing.

When you are ready, get up and go for a walk, taking slow and deliberate steps down the beach. Feel the softness of each step. There is no need to rush; you have all the time you need. With every step, your well-being is enhanced. You feel lighter than ever before.

You now notice that your feet aren't actually on the beach; you are floating gently above the sand. With this sense of freedom, feel yourself rising higher and higher, lighter and lighter, like a balloon floating towards the heavens. You feel completely relaxed and safe. You keep rising higher, feeling so alive, light and safe. You go higher and higher, completely at peace, safe and relaxed.

See yourself seated on a soft cloud, looking down at the beautiful beach from where you just came. To your wonder and delight, you notice how different the beach looks from this new perspective. Look above you and see the stars shining; beneath you the sunshine lights up the beach. This view takes your breath away, as it is the most beautiful thing you have ever seen. The stars are sending to you a beam of starlight which glistens like diamonds. The ocean takes on a shimmering blueness that varies from light to dark—something that you could not see when standing so close. Ah, how wonderful that you have this opportunity to see such contrast: the brightness of the sand, the varying shades of green of the trees. You give thanks for this new vantage point.

It dawns on you that this perspective can also apply to your life, that all which goes on around you each and every day is not always what it seems. Events and situations are occurring, but you need to remove yourself from this situation. Rise above to get the complete picture. The sense of relief that you now have, knowing that there is always another perspective, that all is not what it seems, is life altering. No longer will you come to a conclusion without taking stock and acknowledging this new awareness. You feel so light and alive, ready to take on whatever comes your way.

See yourself standing up. Holding your arms out wide, you take flight and float through the sky between night and day and marvel at this new perspective. Enjoy the sense of freedom that comes with this new gift of yours, the gift of knowing that you can float above any new situation you find yourself in that requires an advantage of seeing the whole picture. Feel the relief; feel the calm; feel the wonder. Feel the lightness.

Keep flying through the sky. You see a soft, very inviting cloud. Notice that there is someone waving to you, inviting you over. As you get closer, you sense that this being is a guide who has something to share. Fly on over, and feel the love as you get closer. This being radiates a beautiful light energy and it permeates you. The love, respect, peace, and trust you feel will remain with you forever.

Take time now to enjoy this energy and to feel the message that is coming to you. Trust that the words which follow are perfect for you right now. Allow and embrace whatever comes into your mind; it is what you need to hear right now.

Take five to ten minutes for reflection.

It is now time to return to the beach. Thank your guide for the wisdom and guidance that he lovingly shared, knowing that you can come back here any time you like. He is with you always and will be waiting for you. Step off the cloud and gently float back to the beach, taking your time and imprinting the magnificent view into your memory. Float back slowly and as you get closer, take a deep breath of the universal energy filling every cell of your body. Feel regenerated, electric and alive. Move your feet from side to side and wiggle your fingers, feeling more alert with every movement. Return to the room and open your eyes, ready to embrace whatever comes to you. Energised and alert, you are ready to start your day with a sense of wonder, vitality, and appreciation.

"See how nature,—trees, flowers, grass—grow in silence; see the stars, the moon, the sun, how they move in silence. We need silence to be able to touch souls."—Mother Teresa

Sleep Meditation

When getting ready to sleep, make sure that your bedroom is free from clutter and distraction. Cover the TV if there is one in your room. Remove all books from your bedside—preferably remove them from the bedroom completely. Your sleep place should be just a bed, night light and clean bedding. All clothes should be in the wardrobe. The clearer the space, the deeper your sleep. Having a bath or shower before bed will also prepare your body for sleep.

When you are ready to retire for the day, lay down on your bed and take a moment to give thanks for the comfortable bed you have, the clean linen, the fresh air. Also give thanks for the wonderful day you have enjoyed: the company of family, friends, colleagues—whatever the case may be.

Become aware of the comfort of your bed, the warmth of the blankets, the softness of your pillow. Really take notice of all these things that support you and will give you a wonderful, deep sleep for the next six to eight hours. Feel the softness of the bed; feel your head sink into your pillow. Feel the relaxation start to descend upon you.

Close your eyes and visualise a candle flame burning gently. Notice the details of this flame, such as how the colours change from orange to red to blue. Notice the gentle flickering and swaying. Look deeply at this flame and take a slow deep breathe, filling your lungs. Slowly exhale all whilst keeping the image of the flame in your mind's eye. Feel yourself relaxing more with each breathe—in and out, in and out—and keep focused on the candle flame. Relax more and more into the bed, feel more and more relaxed, and with each exhalation release the day from your thoughts. It is now time to prepare for a deep sleep.

Say to yourself that it is your intention to have a very restful sleep and that when you awaken in the morning you will wake up fresh and ready for a new day. Let any thoughts that wander into your mind go; these thoughts can be dealt with later. Now is the time for you to prepare for the best, relaxing sleep.

Putting your focus on the candle flame, see the details in your mind's eye. Breathe slowly in, breathe out, breathe in, and breathe out. See the flame gently swaying in the breeze, changing colours from red to orange to yellow. Look at the detail and feel very relaxed. Keep looking at the flame, and feel yourself sinking into the comfort of your bed. Breathe in, breathe out. ...

Star Meditation

S tart with the breathing in through your nose and out through your mouth.

Do three to four minutes of deep breathing, getting relaxed, starting at your head and working your way down your body. Squeeze and relax your head, neck, shoulders, back, torso, upper legs, lower legs, and feet. All the while visualise a silver light surrounding you. Bask in it.

Imagine you are lying in a hammock, gazing up at a night sky filled with many sparkling stars, shining, glistening, and omitting brilliance like you've never seen before. Really focus on these stars, on the beauty, on the mystery, on the essence of the energy that is being filtered to you.

With every breath in, you are breathing the energy of the universe. Breathe deeply and feel this being absorbed by the cells in your body.

Visualise this energy swirling within you and making you feel light and bright, glowing with the knowledge that you are part of this Universe and the Universe is part of you. Feel yourself expanding and becoming one with this magnificent source. It is such an amazing feeling. You have been created from the same energy.

As you gaze up into the heavens, you notice a very bright star coming towards you. As it gets closer and brighter, a feeling of calm and love and peace grows. The rays of this star start to shine all over you and with this comes an inner knowing that you are a magnificent creation of the Universe. Notice how the light separates and a blue ray of light extends towards you. This light is now right beside you. It disperses into thousands of tiny, tiny lights; just like glowing insects, they surround you. The feeling of love within you is comforting. Look at the lights; they are now coming together and taking the shape of your inner being. It is a sight to behold—this is you, your essence. This wonderful being—your *inner you*—has come to share a beautiful message with you.

Take some time now to be alone with your inner self. Listen to the loving guidance being offered to you. Enjoy this time; you have asked for this and your inner being has been waiting for this opportunity to be with you right now. It is the perfect time for you right now.

Take five to eight minutes of silence.

It is now time to leave your inner being and come back to the room. You know now that you can speak with this loving energy any time you like. All you need to do is be silent and listen to your inner being's guidance. You will know, as the thoughts will be accompanied by a feeling of love. Give thanks for this time. Feel the warmth of emotion between you. Feel the peace and know that this inner being is always with you.

Now slowly become aware of your surroundings. Feel yourself seated in your chair. Take note of how you are feeling. Gently wiggle your fingers and toes. Take a deep breath in and out, becoming more aware of the room and of any people in it. Feeling very relaxed, bring back a sense of knowing with you. What a wonderful experience!

Tree Magic

S ee yourself sitting beneath a majestic old tree. It is hundreds of years old and *so* big. The base is very large and able to support the massive branches that extend high into the sky and out wide. It is extremely solid and you are very safe. There is a slight breeze blowing, leave gently swaying. Dappled light filters through the gaps of branches and extends down and around you. Breathe in the magic energy of this tree.

You can feel this beautiful tree's heart beating in time with yours, with each breath your heart slows to a very rhythmic beat. The energy that is coming from the tree is being channelled into you and you can feel the spirit. It so relaxing and peaceful. In your mind's eye, see the nature spirit that is attached to this tree and the love that is coming to you right into your centre—your heart chakra. A beautiful emerald-green, shimmering, sparkling light is flowing from the heart of this tree into you. Breathe deeply this loving energy. With every breath see the light travelling through your body, being carried by every cell in your bloodstream and being passed to other cells deep within your physical body. It is rejuvenating, healing, uplifting, creating a sense of vigour and aliveness.

With every exhalation you are releasing any fear or sadness that may be deep within you. This emerald energy is repairing and inspiring every cell in your being. See you heart chakra glowing; it's a magnificent green light pulsing in time with your heartbeat. Look at all the beautiful butterflies that are now surrounding you. Look at the flowers that are appearing. This is the power of the Universe. Anything is possible, anything.

It's time for you to relax and allow the healing powers of this wonderful energy to do its magic. Take the next few minutes to enjoy and spend time with the wise spirit from this tree. Listen to the guidance that is being offered with so much love and warmth. Bask in this time; all is perfect.

Take seven to nine minutes for reflection.

It's time to return, but before you do, stand up and wrap your arms as far as you can around this tree. Feel the warmth. You understand that this tree is magic. Its trunk is not hard, as you would expect, but very soft and you become one with this tree just for a moment. You feel so grateful for the healing and the love that has been exchanged.

The Mountain

See yourself surrounded by a magnificent mountain range, where the sunlight is bouncing off the peaks and illuminating the sky. You are standing at the base of a particularly beautiful stone path which winds up and around this mountain; it weaves itself right to the very top. You want to take a step to begin this adventure, but you are frozen with fear and doubt, with thoughts of what might go wrong and what might happen if you don't make it.

Stop and ask yourself why you would want to embark on such a journey. Put your focus on what you will gain, what you will see and what you will feel when you succeed. Too often we allow our doubts and fears to be obstacles that prevent us from getting to the top of our mountain. Our mountain could by anything we desire. However, with misguided beliefs, we make it unattainable; we are not able to see the path that would easily allow us to reach the pinnacle of our dreams.

Look down at your feet and see yourself taking a step. Feel the lightness of moving forward. See how the path lights up showing you the next step to take. Remember that there is no right or wrong path; they just take you in different directions. The ultimate outcome is still the same, you will end up somewhere. It is how you feel about your climb and how difficult or easy you choose to make it.

Keep walking, one step at a time, taking deep breaths, filling your lunges with crisp, fresh air. See, it is so easy to do. You are now halfway there. Stop, take a seat and enjoy the view. Take some time to contemplate on your achievements, your successes. Remember that life really is a series of experiences from which to learn. Enjoy the next few moments to pave your way to the new experience; that experience is being created right now as a result of your decision not to let old beliefs decide your fate.

Take time for reflective contemplation.

Now it is time to return to your surroundings. When you are ready, gently move your feet, your legs and your arms, feeling more alert with each movement. Knowing that the new awareness you are bringing into your now moment gives you a real sense of purpose. Coming back now, you are feeling more alert and ready to embrace whatever you choose to do. Open your eyes. You are now feeling very refreshed and fantastic. Well done. You have a choice: you can experience in joy or in pain. *You get to choose.*

About Marjolyn Noble and Leon Steed

Marjolyn Noble was in a rut and miserable with herself. She felt alone, undesirable, lazy—and had no idea where to turn. Fast forward five years, and Marjolyn has literally transformed herself. Not only is she athletically fit, twenty kilos lighter and blissfully in charge of her life, she's a qualified life coach helping others achieve their goals too.

The key, she says, was to stop blaming life and other people on the unhappiness she once felt. "My turning point was joining a local health club and getting Leon Steed as my personal trainer," she said. "I was eighty-eight kilos, unhappy, and very unfit. I was ready to get out of my sedentary lifestyle and shift some emotional weight."

What she got was a new outlook, new body, and new occupation. "Leon is a qualified sports scientist with his feet on the ground and an uncanny insight into human behaviour," says Marjolyn. "But over the next three years of training together, I discovered a whole different side to him; we had all kinds of discussions about philosophies, spirituality, and mindset.

"I've always been very intuitive, but it got lost somewhere along the way. Ironically, it was Leon's down-to-earth approach that triggered the spiritual side of me big-time."

Today, Marjolyn and Leon are an unlikely business team developing opportunities for "people in a rut" to discover—or rediscover—their passions and innate strength.

"I know what it's like to go off track," says Marjolyn. "Leon was instrumental in me realising I'd begun a cycle of negative thoughts that drew a host of other negative side effects. When I finally challenged my thinking, other areas of my life started to change and open up."

Marjolyn and Leon's first joint venture was to produce a CD of three inspirational meditations in early 2011. Soon after, in her capacity as a life coach, Marjolyn was invited to present mindset theories to a mining company and took Leon along to co-present. "It went so well, we developed a series of goal-setting workshops, and then added regular meditation classes," she said.

Late last year, they developed a "sanctuary" for people seeking a life change—just as Marjolyn had found herself wanting to do a few years earlier.

Marjolyn discovered a love for meditation and the creativity behind composing simple guided visualisations. Together Leon and Marjolyn have compiled a collection of different meditations to assist the listener to relax, release, and create a new beginning.

Printed in the United States
By Bookmasters